AN
UNLIKELY
ADVENT
LEADER GUIDE

An Unlikely Advent:
Extraordinary People of the Christmas Story

An Unlikely Advent
978-1-7910-2897-8
978-1-7910-2896-1 eBook

An Unlikely Advent: DVD
978-1-7910-2900-5

An Unlikely Advent: Leader Guide
978-1-7910-2899-2
978-1-7910-2898-5 eBook

RACHEL BILLUPS

AN UNLIKELY ADVENT

LEADER GUIDE

EXTRAORDINARY PEOPLE OF
THE CHRISTMAS STORY

Abingdon Press | Nashville

An Unlikely Advent:
Extraordinary People of the Christmas Story
Leader Guide

978-1-7910-2899-2

MANUFACTURED IN THE
UNITED STATES OF AMERICA

CONTENTS

ABOUT THE
LEADER GUIDE WRITER

Josh Tinley is a high school math teacher who spent ten years as editor of youth curriculum at The United Methodist Publishing House. He is the author of *Book of Fidgets: A Jot and Doodle Journal for Christian Youth, Kneeling in the End Zone: Spiritual Lessons From the World of Sports*, as well as numerous articles and curriculum pieces. Josh lives outside of Nashville with his wife and three children.

INTRODUCTION

Perhaps more than any other holiday, Christmas is heavy on the decorations. Among the multicolored lights, trees, wreaths, and other seasonal décor, many homes and churches feature a Nativity scene: a re-creation of Jesus's birth consisting of figurines representing people who were present for Jesus's birth or who arrived shortly thereafter.

A typical Nativity scene includes baby Jesus in a manger, Mary and Joseph, some shepherds, one or more angels, three wise men, and an assortment of animals. The scenes have become such a staple of our Christmas celebrations that we can't think of baby Jesus without also thinking of a young boy carrying a sheep and men in long robes carrying gold and incense. Not only do shepherds and magi surround Jesus in our Nativity scenes, but they also are the subject of the songs we sing and the stories we tell to children.

The people who visited baby Jesus have become such an integral part of our Christmas traditions that we seldom stop to ask questions such as: Why did an angel tell shepherds about the birth of the Christ child? What is the significance of magi from the east making the long journey to visit a baby rumored to be a Jewish king? What can these people teach us about our faith and our relationships with God and others?

Introduction

In addition to these well-known Nativity scene figures, there are other people we meet in the story of Jesus's birth whom we rarely if ever see in our Christmas decorations. Before we meet Mary and Joseph, the Gospel of Luke introduces us to Elizabeth and Zechariah, parents of John the Baptist. During Matthew's story of the magi, or wise men, we run into King Herod, the villain of the Christmas story. Like the shepherds and magi, these other figures can teach us important lessons about who we are as children of God and followers of Christ.

This study, which is a companion to *An Unlikely Advent* by Rachel Billups, takes a close look at some of the unlikely people we encounter in the stories about Jesus's birth. It includes four sessions, each of which corresponds to a chapter in Billups's book:

Session 1: What If I Missed It?
Life seldom works out the way that we dream or plan it will. We learn from Elizabeth and Zechariah that God's plans often differ from our plans. But, if we trust God, we will find that God blesses us in unexpected ways.

Session 2: Playing the Villain
King Herod, who ruled over Galilee and Judea at the time of Jesus's birth, was jealous and obsessed with power. This led him to commit unspeakable atrocities. We know that God's grace is available to all people, regardless of what they've done. Since all of us are sinners in need of God's grace, this is good news.

Session 3: A Curious People
Jesus and his family were Jewish and the Gospel writers explain how Jesus was the Messiah that some Jewish people had been waiting for. Early in Jesus's story we meet the magi, who traveled from the east and were not Jewish. The magi teach us that Jesus was a savior not only for his people but for all people.

Session 4: When God Shows Up
Every Nativity scene includes shepherds. Luke tells us that they were the first people, outside of Jesus's family, to hear the good news of his birth. The shepherds had a difficult job and were frightened by the angels' presence but nonetheless responded to God's sign, setting an example for followers of Christ still today.

Each session in this study includes the following:

+ Learning objectives: three or four key takeaways from the session
+ Supplies: a list of materials needed for the session. Most sessions require Bibles, paper, pens or pencils, a whiteboard or large sheet of paper, and a marker
+ Opening activity: an activity that participants can do as they gather to introduce the session or one aspect of the session along with a suggested opening prayer
+ Other activities and discussion prompts: activities and prompts that correspond to sections in Billups's book
+ Closing: suggested discussion questions to wrap up the session and a suggested closing prayer

Thank you for leading this study! May it lead you and your group to not only a deeper appreciation of the Nativity story and its unlikely characters but also to a richer and more robust life as followers of Jesus Christ.

1

What If I Missed It?

Session 1
WHAT IF I MISSED IT?

Luke begins his Gospel with an angel announcing the upcoming birth of a child. The child in question was not Jesus, but John the Baptist, Jesus's relative and friend who helped set the stage for Jesus's ministry. Like the announcement of Jesus's birth, news of John's birth came as a shock to his future parents, Elizabeth and Zechariah, because they were both very old. At one point in their lives they likely expected to have children and likely had dreams for those children. But they had long since set aside those plans and had settled into a life of humbly serving God.

God, however, had not given up on Elizabeth and Zechariah's dream of having children and chose them to be the parents of John the Baptist, who would "prepare the way for the Lord" (Luke 3:4). Likewise, many of us discover that our lives don't turn out the way that we had hoped or planned. But, regardless of our expectations, God still has plans for us. God blesses us and works through us, often in surprising ways.

In this session, which follows the opening chapter of *An Unlikely Advent*, we'll get to know Elizabeth and Zechariah. We'll consider our dreams and the ways that God changes our plans.

Session Objectives

This session's readings and discussion will help participants:

+ Reflect on their dreams and plans for the future and consider how God changes their plans for the better.
+ Learn about Elizabeth and Zechariah, parents of John the Baptist, how they had to change their plans, and how they responded to God's call.
+ Consider what is possible as a result of what we have seen God accomplish through God's people.
+ Explore how God is at work on the "rough edges of our story."

Biblical Foundations

In the time of Herod king of Judea there was a priest named Zechariah, who belonged to the priestly division of Abijah; his wife Elizabeth was also a descendant of Aaron. Both of them were righteous in the sight of God, observing all the Lord's commands and decrees blamelessly. But they were childless because Elizabeth was not able to conceive, and they were both very old.

Once when Zechariah's division was on duty and he was serving as priest before God, he was chosen by lot, according to the custom of the priesthood, to go into the temple of the Lord and burn incense. And when the time for the burning of incense came, all the assembled worshipers were praying outside.

Then an angel of the Lord appeared to him, standing at the right side of the altar of incense. When Zechariah saw him, he was startled and was gripped with fear. But the angel said to him: "Do not be afraid, Zechariah; your prayer has been heard. Your wife Elizabeth will bear you a son, and you are to call him John. He will be a joy and delight to you, and many will rejoice because of his birth, for he will be great in the sight of the Lord. He is never to take wine or other fermented drink, and he will be filled with the Holy Spirit even before he is born. He will bring back many of the people of Israel to the Lord their God. And he will go on before the Lord, in the spirit and power of Elijah, to turn the hearts of the parents to their children and the disobedient to the wisdom of the righteous—to make ready a people prepared for the Lord."

Zechariah asked the angel, "How can I be sure of this? I am an old man and my wife is well along in years."

The angel said to him, "I am Gabriel. I stand in the presence of God, and I have been sent to speak to you and to tell you this good news. And now you will be silent and not able to speak until the day this happens, because you did not believe my words, which will come true at their appointed time."

Meanwhile, the people were waiting for Zechariah and wondering why he stayed so long in the temple. When he came out, he could not speak to them. They realized he had seen a vision in the temple, for he kept making signs to them but remained unable to speak.

When his time of service was completed, he returned home. After this his wife Elizabeth became pregnant and for five months remained in seclusion. "The Lord has done this for me," she said. "In these days he has shown his favor and taken away my disgrace among the people."

Luke 1:5-25

Before Your Session

+ Carefully and prayerfully read this session's Biblical Foundations, more than once. Consult a trusted study Bible or commentary for background information.

+ Also read and study Genesis 16:1-6 and Luke 3:1-3, 7-18.
+ Carefully read the introduction and first chapter of *An Unlikely Advent* by Rachel Billups. Make a note about topics that you have questions about or want to research further.
+ You will need: Bibles for in-person participants and/or screen slides prepared with Scripture texts for sharing (be sure to note which translation you are using); a whiteboard or large sheet of paper, markers, paper, and pens or pencils (if meeting in person).
+ If using the DVD or streaming video in your study, preview the session 1 video segment.

Starting Your Session

As they arrive welcome participants to your study of *An Unlikely Advent* by Rachel Billups. Ask volunteers why they are interested in this study and/or what hopes they have for your time together.

Open your time together by discussing some or all of the following questions:

+ Do you set up a Nativity scene in your home (or in your workplace or somewhere else)?
+ Describe your Nativity scene (or scenes).
+ Do you have any pieces in a Nativity scene that are unusual? If so, what are they?
+ Most Nativity scenes include the Holy Family, shepherds, magi, an angel or two, and assorted livestock. What other figures, if any, would you like to see included in Nativity scenes?
+ We don't typically re-create the birth scenes of other revered historical figures. Why, do you think, have Nativity scenes become such a popular Advent and Christmas decoration?

Opening Prayer

God, thank you for bringing us together for this time of study, discussion, and fellowship. Thank you for the example of the many people we meet in the story of Jesus's birth. During our time together, open our hearts and minds to what we can learn from these people and grow in our faith. Amen.

Video Presentation

Play the first track on the DVD or the streaming session of *An Unlikely Advent*, session 1 (running time is approximately 8–10 minutes). Open the floor for a few minutes of discussion.

Discussion Questions

God-Sized Dreams

+ What were the earliest dreams you remember having about your future and what life would be like when you were older? (This could involve a future career, an idea or invention you wanted to get off the ground, where you might be living or might travel, or something else.)

+ How have these dreams changed as you've gotten older? (Specifically, you might ask: Which dreams have gotten less ambitious? Which have changed drastically? If you've given up on a dream, why? Was it not realistic? Did you become interested in something else?)

+ When have you found yourself wavering and wondering if your dreams are even possible? What causes you to doubt your dreams?

+ Billups writes about her mother having to let go of her dream to become a missionary because, "sometimes life

17

happens." When has life happened to you, disrupting your plans and dreams?

+   What dreams do you now have for your future?
    Do you think that these dreams are more or less realistic or attainable than those you had when you were young? Why, or why not?

+   How open are you to changing your plans and pursuing new dreams?

Giving Up on Your Dreams

Invite a volunteer to read aloud Luke 1:5-10.

+   The Advent season is a season of waiting. What things have you had to wait for? What is the longest that you have had to wait for something?

+   What is most difficult about waiting?

+   What do these verses tell us about Elizabeth and Zechariah?

+   What dreams might Elizabeth and Zechariah have had? What dreams or plans might they have changed or given up on?

+   Billups writes about Elizabeth and Zechariah, "I imagine that through the decades this faith-filled couple was wondering, *What if we missed it?*" (page 8). When have you wondered if you missed out on something or if an opportunity had passed you by? How did you deal with this disappointment?

+   Billups writes, "We totally can honor the past and celebrate our achievements. But when the past becomes the pinnacle of the present, we find ourselves paralyzed, staring into a future without possibilities" (page 10). What are the dangers of dwelling on the past and worrying about whether you've missed out on something?

+ Billups refers to a neuroscientist who suggested that our brains are resistant to change. When have you been afraid of change? When have you overcome this tendency by embracing change?
+ Luke 1:6 tells us that Elizabeth and Zechariah "were righteous in the sight of God, observing all the Lord's commands and decrees blamelessly." Despite the disappointments they'd suffered, Elizabeth and Zechariah remained faithful to God. How do you remain focused on your faith and on God's will during times of waiting and disappointment?
+ Invite another volunteer to read aloud Luke 1:12-18.
+ How does Zechariah react to seeing the angel? How does Zechariah respond to the news that he will be a father?
+ How, do you think, would you have reacted to the angel's announcement if you'd been in Elizabeth or Zechariah's position?
+ Why, do you think, did God choose this couple instead of a younger couple to be the parents of God's messenger?
+ When have you abruptly had to change your plans? What sacrifices did you have to make or what challenges did you have to overcome?

Scared Speechless

+ Invite a volunteer to read aloud Luke 1:18-23.
+ Zechariah was a priest known for his righteousness and faithfulness. Yet, when the angel of the Lord appeared to him, he was "startled and was gripped with fear" (Luke 1:12). What, do you think, was so frightening about the angel?
+ Billups writes, "Sometimes we too get so caught up in the religious routine that we forget to expect the unexpected"

(page 13). What, do you think, does it mean to "expect the unexpected"?

+ Second Timothy 1:7 in the NRSVue says, "God did not give us a spirit of cowardice but rather a spirit of power and of love and of self-discipline." How do love and self-discipline equip us to be courageous when we face unexpected news and challenges?

+ When, if ever, is it okay to be afraid?

+ How can fear keep us from the blessings and opportunities that God has in store for us?

Cracks Are Where the Light Floods In

+ Elizabeth and Zechariah's story parallels the story of Abram and Sarai (later Abraham and Sarah) in the Book of Genesis. Abram was seventy-five and he and Sarai childless, yet God promised that they would be parents of a great nation. Read Genesis 16:1-6. How did Abram and Sarai take matters into their own hands? Who was hurt as a result?

+ When God made a promise to Abram and Sarai, they followed God's instructions by moving from Ur to Canaan. Twenty-five years later Sarai, now Sarah, still had not given birth to the child God had promised. When have you waited expectantly for something that seemed like it would never happen? Did you give up? If not, how did you stay hopeful?

+ Read Genesis 18:1-15. How did God appear to Abraham? What message did God have for Abraham? How did Abraham and Sarah respond to the visitors?

+ What can we gain from the "rough edges of our story"? How can "pain and confusion" help us "see the beauty and experience the good" (page 15)?

+ God was faithful to Abraham and Sarah. Sarah gave birth to a son, Isaac, despite her old age. What can we learn from Abraham and Sarah about trusting God amid frustration and uncertainty?

Set Your Hopes High

+ What do you know about the meaning of your name? (This could involve the meaning of your name in its language of origin or the reason why your parents chose this name for you.)

+ If you have had opportunities to choose names (whether for children, for pets, for yourself, or for someone or something else), how have you decided on them? How important was it that the names be meaningful?

+ Read aloud Luke 1:57-64. Why do Elizabeth and Zechariah go against tradition by naming their son John?

+ *John* in Hebrew means "God is gracious." What does it mean for God to be gracious? How have you experienced God's grace? How did Elizabeth and Zechariah experience God's grace?

+ Look back at Luke 1:13-15. What expectations does God have for John the Baptist? Why, do you think, does God have these high expectations for John? (*Note:* This commitment to avoid all fermented drinks is part of the Nazirite vow described in Numbers 6. Nazirites—not to be confused with Nazarenes, or people from Nazareth—made a commitment to holiness and avoiding certain behaviors. John may have been a Nazirite.)

+ Read aloud Luke 3:1-3, 7-18. John, Elizabeth and Zechariah's long-awaited child, played an important role in Jesus's ministry. What do these verses tell us about John?

+ What does it mean that John prepared the way for Jesus? How did he do this?

Dream Forward

+ What, do you think, does Billups mean by "teaching our people how to dream" (page 25)?
+ One way to teach people to dream is to show them what is possible. How does our congregation show people what is possible with God?
+ Billups asks whether "our people have permission to dream forward" (page 25). How might we, without intending to, discourage people from dreaming or pursuing "God possibilities"?
+ How do we, or can we, equip people to pursue their dreams? (For instance, how does, or should, a congregation support new ministries and give people the tools they need to make those ministries successful?)

Contagious Hope

+ Billups mentions a conversation with a Palestinian Christian who was frustrated by "blind faith" among American Christians. He said, "Hatred is fueled by blind faith" (page 28). What is blind faith? How might blind faith fuel hatred?
+ How do we embrace a faith that is not blind but that is grounded in experience?
+ What are some situations or challenges in our world that are particularly difficult to be hopeful about?
+ Considering the situations and challenges in the previous question, what have you seen or experienced that gives you hope for the future?

   ✦   Billups writes, "Hope is contagious.... When we listen to one another's stories…It gifts us hope and, in the process, we are changed. We begin to believe that if God can rewrite the stories of other people, God can rewrite our unlikely stories as well" (pages 28–29). What stories have given you hope?

Optional Activity

Write the following statement, with the blanks, on a whiteboard or large sheet of paper.

I have hope that _____

because _____.

Hand out paper. Then instruct participants to fill out this statement as many times as they'd like by identifying a) something they are hopeful for and b) a reason why they are hopeful that this thing can happen.

For example, "I have hope that we can raise money to pay for our upcoming mission work because I have seen our congregation come together to make things happen"; or "I have hope that there will be a cure for cancer in my lifetime because I know how much progress has been made in medical research in recent decades." These statements can express hope for things that are personal (such as a group or team you're a part of achieving a goal) or global (such as ending hunger or eradicating diseases). For all of these hopes, focus on *what you see other people doing* that gives you hope.

Allow participants a few minutes to work. Then allow everyone to read aloud one or more of their statements.

Discuss:

   ✦   What is a statement from another person in this group (not yourself) that makes you especially hopeful?

Your Unlikely Story

- Billups writes, "God is no cosmic Santa Claus. Humans do not receive everything we have ever wanted, yet there are dreams in our head and in our hearts that God wants to creatively partner with us to make happen" (page 30). What, do you think, does she mean by saying that God is not a "cosmic Santa Claus"?
- While God doesn't give us everything we ask for, God blesses us and gives us gifts, even if they aren't always the gifts we want or expect. What gifts has God given you? How can you use these gifts in service of God and others?
- What can we learn from the example of Elizabeth and Zechariah about God's gifts and how God makes dreams a reality?

Closing

Discuss:

- What is one thing you learned during our time together that you didn't know before?
- What is one thing that you will do in the coming week as a result of what we learned or discussed?

Closing Prayer

God, thank you for bringing us together for this time of study and discussion. We know from the story of Elizabeth and Zechariah that, through you, all things are possible. Open our hearts and minds, eyes and ears, to all the ways that we can answer your call even if it requires us to change our plans. In Christ's name we pray. Amen.

2

Playing
the Villain

Session 2
PLAYING THE VILLAIN

Most great stories include a villain. This is certainly true of the Christmas story. At the time of Jesus's birth, King Herod the Great ruled over Galilee (Mary and Joseph's homeland) and Judea (Joseph's ancestral home and where Jesus was born). Herod considered himself the king of the Jews, but his power came not from the Jewish people but from the Roman emperor. He had a reputation for cruelty and was more interested in his power and legacy than in Jewish faith and tradition.

Matthew's Gospel tells us that Herod felt threatened when he heard people refer to Jesus—who was only a baby—as a savior and king. To eliminate this supposed threat, Herod ordered the massacre of all young children in the Bethlehem area. While Jesus and his family were safe, hiding away in Egypt, many other children were victims of this unspeakable evil.

It's easy for us to condemn Herod. There's no question that he was power-hungry and wicked. It's much harder for us to come to terms with the fact that, in spite of everything Herod did, God's love and grace is still available to him. We confess that we are also sinners. Like Herod, we are in need of redemption.

In this session, which follows the second chapter of *An Unlikely Advent*, we'll learn about Herod. And we'll consider how God's love and grace is for all people, no matter what.

Session Objectives

This session's readings and discussion will help participants:

+ Learn about King Herod, ruler of Judea and Galilee at the time of Jesus's birth.
+ Consider how jealousy and selfishness have negative effects on our lives and relationships.
+ Struggle with the truth that God's love and grace is for all people, even those who do horrible things.
+ Recognize that we too are in need of God's love and grace.

Biblical Foundations

After Jesus was born in Bethlehem in Judea, during the time of King Herod, Magi from the east came to Jerusalem and asked, "Where is the one who has been born king of the Jews? We saw his star when it rose and have come to worship him."

When King Herod heard this he was disturbed, and all Jerusalem with him....

Then Herod called the Magi secretly and found out from them the exact time the star had appeared. He sent them to Bethlehem and said, "Go and search carefully for the child. As soon as you find him, report to me, so that I too may go and worship him."...

When they had gone, an angel of the Lord appeared to Joseph in a dream. "Get up," he said, "take the child and his mother and escape to Egypt. Stay there until I tell you, for Herod is going to search for the child to kill him."...

When Herod realized that he had been outwitted by the Magi, he was furious, and he gave orders to kill all the boys in Bethlehem and its vicinity who were two years old and under, in accordance with the time he had learned from the Magi.

Matthew 2:1-3, 7-8, 13, 16

Before Your Session

+ Carefully and prayerfully read this session's Biblical Foundations, more than once. Consult a trusted study Bible or commentary for background information.
+ Also read and study 1 Kings 18:22-40; Matthew 1:1-17; John 3:1-18; and Romans 3:23-24.
+ Carefully read the second chapter of *An Unlikely Advent* by Rachel Billups. Make a note about topics that you have questions about or want to research further.
+ You will need: Bibles for in-person participants and/or screen slides prepared with Scripture texts for sharing.
+ If using the DVD or streaming video in your study, preview the session 2 video segment.

Starting Your Session

Welcome participants back to your study of *An Unlikely Advent.* As they arrive, discuss:

+ Who are some fictional characters whom you find particularly difficult to love?
+ If you had to, could you identify at least one positive quality of each of these characters? (This might be the love that he or she shows to someone else, a special talent he or she has, or an admirable trait.)

+ Why are villains so important in storytelling?
+ Which villains from fiction or history have the best redemption narratives?

Opening Prayer

God, thank you for bringing us back together for this time of study, discussion, and fellowship. Watch over us as we discuss people who we consider villains and who are often difficult for us to love. Open our hearts and minds to the message you have for us today. Amen.

Video Presentation

Play the first track on the DVD or the streaming session of *An Unlikely Advent*, session 2 (running time is approximately 8–10 minutes). Open the floor for a few minutes of discussion.

Discussion Questions

Nobody Loves a Villain

+ Read through Matthew 1:1-17. How does Matthew begin his Gospel? What familiar names do you see in this lineage?
+ Jesus's genealogy includes kings such as David, Solomon, and Josiah. How does Jesus's birth and upbringing differ from what we'd normally associate with royalty?
+ What do you know about King Herod the Great, the king of Galilee and Judea at the time of Jesus's birth?

Ask a participant to read aloud Matthew 2:1-3, 7-8, 13, and 16.

+ What assumptions might Herod have made about Jesus based on what the magi told him?

- Based on his actions in these verses, how would you describe Herod?
- Billups writes, "Cruel, paranoid, and seemingly senseless in his violence, Herod lived by the myth of redemptive violence and believed that the strongest arm ruled by divine destiny" (page 39). Herod's power and authority came from the Roman emperor. Why would Rome put a cruel tyrant in charge of its territories? (You might mention that Rome was interested in maintaining *Pax Romana*, or Roman Peace. The empire guaranteed security and stability for its territories, but the people in the territories had to play by Roman rules.)
- Matthew tells us that Herod had his soldiers kill all the children near Bethlehem. This story does not appear in other sources. Billups notes, "The historical evidence of such an act was unclear, but these actions certainly were in alignment with Herod's character and past behavior" (page 40). Aside from what it tells us about Herod, what is the significance of this story? What does it tell us about Jesus? (You might discuss the parallels between Jesus and Moses and between Herod's massacre and Pharaoh's massacre of the Hebrew babies born in Egypt.)

A Herod in Us All

- Billups writes that one thing we possibly all have in common is that we have "treated another human being as less than human" (page 42). For what reasons do we have this tendency to dehumanize other people?
- Why—or in what circumstances—does it feel good to put down or embarrass other people?

+ When have you struggled with jealousy? When has jealously caused you to do something that you would later regret?

Ask volunteers to read aloud 1 Kings 18:22-40.

+ What does this Scripture tell us about Elijah?
+ Read 1 Kings 19:1-5. In just a few verses, Elijah goes from confidently defeating 450 prophets of the Canaanite god Baal to fearing for his life. What happened to Elijah?
+ Billups mentions the words "limitation prophecy": When we hear negative messages about what isn't possible and what we're not capable of, we internalize them and they place limitations on what we can actually do. How was Elijah a victim of a limitation prophecy?
+ When have you been a victim of a limitation prophecy? When have you spoken a limitation prophecy to someone else?

The Scandal of Love

Invite a participant to read aloud John 3:1-18.

+ Billups writes, "We struggle with God's scandalous love embodied in Jesus" (page 49). What, do you think, does she mean by, "God's scandalous love embodied in Jesus"?
+ How is God's "scandalous love" at work in these verses in John 3?
+ Why, do you think, does Nicodemus go to see Jesus at night? What does Nicodemus find interesting or curious about Jesus?
+ John 3:16, one of the Bible's best-known and most beloved verses, is part of Jesus's response to Nicodemus. Why, do you think, has this verse become such a popular verse for those who want to promote the Christian faith?

- As with any Scripture, it's important that we put John 3:16 into context. What does John 3:17 add to Jesus's words in the previous verse? What do these verses, together, tell us about God?
- What, do you think, does Jesus mean when he talks about God saving the world? What does it mean for the world to be saved?
- What does God's scandalous love mean for someone like Herod?
- What does God's scandalous love mean for us and our attitudes and behaviors toward other people?

Real Life Herods

Billups, in *An Unlikely Advent*, tells a story about a man named Stan whom she met through the Kindway organization. As a seventeen-year-old Stan murdered someone and spent the next thirty-four years in jail. In jail his violent and destructive behavior continued. After reluctantly attending a four-day retreat while he was a prisoner, Stan experienced God's scandalous love, a love that completely transformed him.

Ask volunteers to read aloud Stan's story, a paragraph or two at a time, from pages 51–54 in *An Unlikely Advent*.

- What parts of Stan's story do you relate to the most?
- What parts of Stan's story do you struggle with or have questions about?
- Jesus teaches in Matthew 25:40 that when we serve "the least of these"—which includes prisoners—we serve him. Jesus sees himself in people who are suffering and vulnerable and who have been rejected by others. How do you see Jesus in Stan?

- How did Stan's transformation have a positive impact on other people? How would things have been different if God had given up on Stan and cast him aside?
- Though he experienced transformation and redemption, Stan had hurt people very badly. How do we acknowledge God's scandalous love and grace without excusing or dismissing the hurt that people have caused?

Your Unlikely Story

A participant should read aloud Romans 3:23-24.

- How do these verses from Paul's letter to the Christians in Rome relate to our discussion about God's scandalous love?
- When in your life have you played the villain? Did you recognize at the time that you were in the wrong, or did you realize it later? (It is okay if participants are not comfortable answering this question.)
- What have you learned from these experiences when you were the villain? How have you changed or grown as a result of these experiences?

Closing

Discuss:

- What is one thing you learned during our time together that you didn't know before?
- What is one thing that you will do in the coming week as a result of what we learned or discussed?

Closing Prayer

God, thank you for bringing us together for this time of study and discussion. We know that you love all of us, despite our shortcomings. Give us the strength and courage to show that same love and grace to all people, especially those who are difficult for us to love. Open our eyes to the ways that we fall short and hurt others so that we may learn and grow and become the people you call us to be. In Christ's name we pray. Amen.

3

A Curious People

Session 3
A CURIOUS PEOPLE

Most every Nativity scene includes wise men, or magi—usually three of them. Matthew tells us that the magi came from the east and brought gifts of gold, frankincense, and myrrh. Anything more than that is speculation.

The magi are important for a couple reasons. For one, they began the tradition of giving gifts at Christmas. And their gifts tell us something about Jesus: Gold is a gift fit for a king; frankincense, when burned, rises to the heavens and signifies Jesus's divinity; myrrh, which can be used to prepare bodies for burial, reminds us that Jesus is also fully human and died a human death.

As much as everyone loves to give and receive presents, the magi serve a more important function. They are outsiders. They are not Jewish and do not understand Jewish ideas about a messiah. They don't understand the significance of Jesus being born in Bethlehem, the hometown of King David. But they know there is something special about Jesus. The magi show us—very early in Jesus's life—that Jesus's ministry, death, and resurrection are not only for his fellow Jewish people but for all people, regardless of culture or nationality.

The wise men remind us to reach out to those who might be considered outsiders in our congregations and communities. God calls us to invite and welcome these people.

In this session, which follows the third chapter of *An Unlikely Advent*, we'll meet the magi. And we'll consider how our congregation can be a place where people of different cultures and backgrounds can feel comfortable.

Session Objectives

This session's readings and discussion will help participants:

+ Consider why gift-giving is a part of Christmas traditions and reflect on the gifts that the magi brought to Jesus.
+ Examine the importance of the town of Bethlehem to the ancient Israelites and to the Jewish people at the time of Jesus.
+ Explore what we can learn from the magi about Jesus and how God's grace is available to all people.
+ Discuss how your congregation can become more welcoming and inviting for people who might feel like outsiders.

Biblical Foundations

After Jesus was born in Bethlehem in Judea, during the time of King Herod, Magi from the east came to Jerusalem and asked, "Where is the one who has been born king of the Jews? We saw his star when it rose and have come to worship him." ...

Then Herod called the Magi secretly and found out from them the exact time the star had appeared. He sent them to Bethlehem and said, "Go and search carefully for the child. As soon as you find him, report to me, so that I too may go and worship him."

After they had heard the king, they went on their way, and the star they had seen when it rose went ahead of them until it stopped over the place where the child was. When they saw the star, they were overjoyed. On coming to the house, they saw the child with his mother Mary, and they bowed down and worshiped him. Then they opened their treasures and presented him with gifts of gold, frankincense and myrrh. And having been warned in a dream not to go back to Herod, they returned to their country by another route.

Matthew 2:1-2, 7-12

Before Your Session

+   Carefully and prayerfully read this session's Biblical Foundations, more than once. Consult a trusted study Bible or commentary for background information.
+   Also read and study Micah 5:1-4.
+   Carefully read the third chapter of *An Unlikely Advent* by Rachel Billups. Make a note about topics that you have questions about or want to research further.
+   You will need: Bibles for in-person participants and/or screen slides prepared with Scripture texts for sharing.
+   If using the DVD or streaming video in your study, preview the session 3 video segment.

Starting Your Session

Welcome participants back to your study of *An Unlikely Advent*. As they arrive, discuss:

+   When do you start celebrating the buildup to Christmas? How early do you decorate your house? When do you usually start listening to Christmas music?

+ When, do you think, is it appropriate for businesses to put up Christmas decorations and start playing Christmas music? Does it bother you when businesses decorate or play Christmas music when you consider it too early?
+ Why, do you think, do we start celebrating and preparing for Christmas so early, especially when compared to other holidays? What is so exciting about the holiday season?
+ For many people, particularly children, much of the anticipation for Christmas is about presents. How has your attitude about receiving and giving Christmas presents changed over the years?

Opening Prayer

God, thank you for bringing us back together for this time of study, discussion, and fellowship. Watch over us as we anticipate this year's Christmas celebration and reflect on gifts—those you've given us and those that we can give to others. Open our hearts and minds to what we can learn from the magi who brought unlikely gifts to the Christ child many years ago. We pray these things in Christ's name. Amen.

Video Presentation

Play the first track on the DVD or the streaming session of *An Unlikely Advent*, session 3 (running time is approximately 8–10 minutes). Open the floor for a few minutes of discussion.

Discussion Questions

An Unlikely Gift

Ask a volunteer to read aloud Matthew 2:7-12.

* Why, do you think, is gift-giving such a key part of our Christmas celebrations?

* What was the most meaningful gift you've ever received for Christmas? What made this gift so special? Was this a gift that you'd been looking forward to or was it a surprise?

* Our tradition of giving gifts at Christmas recalls the time when Jesus received, in Billups's words, "an unlikely gift from a curious people" (page 65). The mysterious magi from the east brought Jesus gifts of gold, frankincense, and myrrh when they visited him as a baby. What, do you think, is the significance of the magi bringing Jesus gold?

* What do you know about frankincense and myrrh? For what reasons might frankincense and myrrh be unusual gifts for a baby?

◊ As needed provide the following information about frankincense and myrrh.

◊ **Frankincense** is a resin obtained from certain tropical trees that is used in perfumes and incense. In Leviticus 2:1, God's people are instructed to include frankincense with their grain offerings so that their offerings, when burned, will have a pleasant aroma. Traditionally, frankincense is a reminder of Jesus's divinity because the smoke of burning incense rises to heaven.

◊ **Myrrh**, like frankincense, is a resin. It is extracted from certain short, thorny trees. Myrrh is also used in incense, and Esther 2:12 refers to a purification rule involving myrrh oil. The Gospel of John tells us that, following the crucifixion, Jesus's friend and follower Nicodemus brought myrrh to Jesus's tomb to anoint the body. Because of this association with burial, myrrh traditionally reminds us of Jesus's humanity. Though he was God, Jesus was also fully human and died a human death.

◊   *Note*: As frankincense represents the divinity of Jesus and myrrh represents his humanity, gold traditionally reminds us of his royalty.

✦   Read Psalm 72:10-11 and Isaiah 60:6. What do these verses have to say about the gifts the magi brought Jesus?

✦   Burning incense is a spiritual practice and part of worship in some Christian traditions. What is your experience with incense in worship? How can engaging the senses, such as with the aroma of burning incense, draw us closer to God and focus our hearts and minds on the Holy Spirit?

✦   Why, do you think, does Matthew tell us that the magi brought these gifts? Do these gifts tell us anything about the magi, or about Jesus?

A Peculiar Place

✦   What do you know about the town of Bethlehem (either today or in biblical times)?

Ask a participant to read aloud the first three paragraphs of the "A Peculiar Place" section of chapter 3 (page 69) of *An Unlikely Advent*.

✦   What was peculiar about Bethlehem? Why might the fact that Jesus was born in Bethlehem have been an embarrassment to his early followers?

✦   Billups tells a story about a classmate learning that she had come from the small town of Laurelville, Ohio. The classmate said to her, "Rachel, there is no way you are from Laurelville. You are too smart to be from

Laurelville" (page 72). When have you been surprised
to learn where someone was born or grew up? Why
were you surprised? Why do we have stereotypes and
expectations related to where people are from?

+ What assumptions have people made about you based on
your birthplace or hometown? How do you respond to
criticisms about where you are from?

+ Billups mentions that some scholars think that the choice
of Bethlehem as Jesus's birthplace was an "invention of the
Gospel writers" (page 69). Why would the Gospel writers
(specifically Matthew and Luke) have landed on Bethlehem
when trying to determine Jesus's birthplace? What was special
about Bethlehem? (As needed, point out that Bethlehem was
the hometown of King David, Israel's most important king.)

+ What does it tell us about Jesus that God didn't choose for
him to be born in an important city such as Rome, or even
Jerusalem?

+ Read Matthew 2:3-6. These verses refer back to Micah 5:1-4
in the Old Testament. What does Micah have to say about
Bethlehem?

+ Micah was speaking to people in his time, hundreds of years
before Jesus, who were worried about threats from powerful
neighboring empires. Micah was not describing Jesus, but
Matthew saw parallels between Christ and Micah's "ruler
of Israel" from Bethlehem. How does this ruler of Israel,
described in verses 3 and 4, remind you of Jesus?

A Curious People

+ What comes to mind when you think of the magi, or wise
men? How would you describe the wise men that appear in
Nativity scenes and Christmas pageants?

Then invite a volunteer to read aloud Matthew 2:1-2, 7-11.

+ What differences did you notice between our descriptions of the magi and what Scripture actually tells us about the magi?

+ What are some things that we often assume about the magi that don't come from the Bible? (Tradition tells us that there were three magi, because they brought three gifts. Matthew doesn't actually give us a number. Over time, the church even gave the magi the names Caspar, Balthasar, and Melchior. These names are not found in Scripture.)

+ The magi likely did not visit Jesus when he was an infant. Billups suggests that the magi probably visited a toddler Jesus. In your experience, how do toddlers respond to receiving gifts? How do they respond to meeting new people?

Ask a volunteer to read aloud the following from *An Unlikely Advent* (page 75):

> *These magi were not exactly kings.... The Greek word for magi, "magos," can mean wise men, astrologers, priests, but also magician or sorcerers as well.*[1] *... The magi are a bit odd. At first glance, they seem like pagan performers, outside of the people of God.*

+ When have you felt like an outsider?

+ Why might someone feel like an outsider in our congregation, or as a part of this group?

+ In what ways might people get the impression that they don't really belong in our congregation or that they aren't

---

1   M. Eugene Boring, "Matthew" in *The New Interpreter's Bible Commentary*, vol 7 (Nashville: Abingdon Press, 2015), 77.

really welcome? (Think of ways that we might exclude or push away people without meaning to.)

+ What might seem strange or confusing to someone visiting our church for the first time, especially if that person was not from a Christian background?

+ What could we do to make our congregation more welcoming to visitors from different religious or cultural backgrounds?

Your Unlikely Story

Have participants stand in the middle of the room. Designate one end of the room, "Strongly agree." Designate the other, "Strongly disagree."

Read aloud each of the following statements. After each one, participants should move somewhere in the room to indicate how much they agree or disagree with the statement. (The more strongly they agree, the closer they should move to the "strongly agree" side.)

Statements:

+ I enjoy meeting new people.
+ I enjoy visiting and worshipping with other congregations.
+ As followers of Christ, we have a responsibility to invite people—especially our friends and family—to worship with us.
+ There is something about Christmas season worship services that make them more special than most other worship services.
+ After participants move in response to each statement, invite volunteers to explain why they chose to move where they did.

Then discuss:

+ We see early on in Jesus's story that the good news of Jesus is good news for all people. What do you find most challenging about sharing the good news of Jesus with others?
+ In what situations are you most comfortable inviting people to worship or share your faith?
+ Billups says of Christmas Eve worship, "I have witnessed Christmas Eve become a spiritual catalyst in people's lives" (page 83). What, do you think, does she mean by this?
+ Many churches see a surge in attendance during the Advent and Christmas seasons, and especially at Christmas Eve services. What do you find most compelling about Christmas worship?
+ What could we do, as a group or as a congregation, to welcome Christmas visitors to continue worshipping with us or to encourage them in their spiritual journey?
+ How might you be able to use the gifts and opportunities available to you to invite or welcome people to the faith community?
+ The magi brought gifts to the Christ child. What gifts have new members brought into our congregation?
+ What gifts might we miss out on if we don't welcome outsiders?

Closing

Discuss:

+ What is one thing you learned during our time together that you didn't know before?

+ What is one thing that you will do in the coming week as a result of what we learned or discussed?

Closing Prayer

God, thank you for bringing us together for this time of study and discussion. Thank you for the witness and example of the magi. Work through us to show your love and grace to all people, including those outside the community of faith. In Christ's name we pray. Amen

4

When God
Shows Up

Session 4
WHEN GOD SHOWS UP

Sometimes, amid the busyness and stress of our lives, we want a sign. We want God to tell us what to do or to show us that we're on the right track. Signs from God are a big part of the Christmas story. Mary, Joseph, and Zechariah got visits from angels. The magi followed a star in the sky. And the shepherds got a concert from a heavenly host.

For the shepherds, receiving a sign from God was shocking and frightening. Their job of tending and protecting sheep was already dangerous; receiving messages from strange beings in the middle of the night only added to the anxiety that the shepherds were already feeling.

A group of shepherds had no reason to think that they would be chosen by God to hear a special announcement. While their work was essential, it didn't offer much in the way of wealth, power, and glory. Shepherds were common people. Yet shepherds were the people whom God chose to be the first to meet the Christ child.

Throughout Jesus's story and the story of the early church, we see examples of the Holy Spirit working through unlikely people. We know that God continues to be present with us in the person of the Holy Spirit. The Spirit moves through us; we just need to slow down and allow ourselves to focus.

In this session, which follows the fourth chapter of *An Unlikely Advent*, we'll get to know the shepherds. And we'll consider how, through prayer and meditation, we can focus on the work of God's Holy Spirit.

Session Objectives

This session's readings and discussion will help participants:

+ Consider the signs that God gives us and how these signs challenge us.
+ Look at the example of the shepherds who, despite being afraid and anxious, were the first people outside of Jesus's family to hear the good news of his birth.
+ Discuss who in our community, like the shepherds, is overlooked, despite doing difficult and essential work.
+ Focus on how the Holy Spirit is at work in our lives, especially during times of stress and difficulty.

Biblical Foundations

And there were shepherds living out in the fields nearby, keeping watch over their flocks at night. An angel of the Lord appeared to them, and the glory of the Lord shone around them, and they were terrified. But the angel said to them, "Do not be afraid. I bring you good news that will cause great joy for all the people. Today in the town of David a Savior has been born to you; he is the Messiah, the Lord. This will be a sign to you: You will find a baby wrapped in cloths and lying in a manger."

Suddenly a great company of the heavenly host appeared with the angel, praising God and saying,

"Glory to God in the highest heaven,
and on earth peace to those on whom his favor rests."

When the angels had left them and gone into heaven, the shepherds said to one another, "Let's go to Bethlehem and see this thing that has happened, which the Lord has told us about."

So they hurried off and found Mary and Joseph, and the baby, who was lying in the manger. When they had seen him, they spread the word concerning what had been told them about this child, and all who heard it were amazed at what the shepherds said to them. But Mary treasured up all these things and pondered them in her heart. The shepherds returned, glorifying and praising God for all the things they had heard and seen, which were just as they had been told.

Luke 2:8-20

Before Your Session

+ Carefully and prayerfully read this session's Biblical Foundations, more than once. Consult a trusted study Bible or commentary for background information.
+ Also read and study Psalm 23; Matthew 11:28-29; John 10:10-18; and Acts 9:36-43.
+ Carefully read the fourth chapter of *An Unlikely Advent* by Rachel Billups. Make a note about topics that you have questions about or want to research further.
+ You will need: Bibles for in-person participants and/or screen slides prepared with Scripture texts for sharing.
+ If using the DVD or streaming video in your study, preview the session 4 video segment.

Starting Your Session

Welcome participants back to your study of *An Unlikely Advent*. As they arrive, discuss:

- What causes you the most stress during the Advent season and the lead-up to Christmas? In terms of stress, how does this time of year compare to others in terms of anxiety?
- How does stress affect your mood and attitude during Advent and Christmas? How does it affect your spiritual practices and your relationship with God? What does your stress cause you to miss out on?
- Where do you find peace during the holiday season?
- Read Matthew 11:28-29. In what ways can you, or do you, find rest in Jesus? How does Jesus lighten your burden?
- What things might you be able to do (or not do) so that Advent and Christmas will be less stressful for you and your loved ones?

Opening Prayer

God, thank you for bringing us back together for this time of study, discussion, and fellowship. Take our anxiety and stress so that we can focus our hearts and minds on you, on one another, and on the message that you have for us during this season. We pray these things in Christ's name. Amen.

Video Presentation

Play the first track on the DVD or the streaming session of *An Unlikely Advent*, session 4 (running time is approximately 8-10 minutes). Open the floor for a few minutes of discussion.

Discussion Questions

Looking for a Sign

+ Billups writes, "We want signs. We long for guideposts along life's journey to reassure us that we are not messing up" (page 91). When have you wanted a sign? When have you needed some assurance that you were on the track or some indication of what decision you should make?

+ What sorts of signs are we looking for? When you are desperate for clarity or validation, what sorts of signals do you hope to see or hear?

+ When have you seen a sign that gave you hope or helped you make an important decision?

Invite volunteers to read aloud Luke 2:8-14.

+ What were the angel's first words to the shepherds? What, do you think, was frightening about the angel and the "glory of the Lord" that "shone around them"? What, do you imagine, did the angel who appeared to the shepherds look like?

+ Put yourself in the shepherds' position. How, do you think, would you have responded to the angel's news? Specifically, how might you have reacted to the news that the person being described as your "Savior" was a newborn baby?

+ Reread verses 13 and 14. How do you picture this scene?

+ After this experience with God's messengers, what expectations, do you think, did the shepherds have? What questions might they have had?

+ Earlier we discussed how stressful the lead-up to Christmas can be. What, do you think, caused the shepherds stress on this night when they learned of Jesus's birth?

+ What do you know about the shepherds who visited Jesus?

Ask a participant to read aloud this passage from *An Unlikely Advent* describing the shepherds on pages 92–93:

> *They were third-shift workers in charge of watching of sheep in the town of Bethlehem through the night. They had a job to do....As part of the working class, shepherds had a mixed reputation. When it comes to the socioeconomic ladder, these guys were near the bottom.*

+ How does this description of the shepherds compare with how we present shepherds in Nativity scenes and Christmas pageants?
+ Billups writes, "Why would the God of the universe choose shepherds as primary witnesses to the birth of the Savior of the world? Why make this announcement; why give this sign to a strange group of shepherds?" What do you think? Why did God choose the shepherds?

Ask a participant to read aloud Psalm 23.

+ What is the psalmist saying about God by referring to God as a shepherd? How is calling God a shepherd different from referring to God as a lord or king?

Invite another participant to read aloud John 10:11-18.

+ Jesus describes himself as a shepherd. What does this tell us about Jesus and what kind of a messiah he is?
+ David worked as a shepherd before he was anointed King of Israel. Moses was working as a shepherd when God called him to deliver the Israelites from slavery in Egypt. Why, do you think, is there such a strong connection between shepherding and those whom God chooses as leaders?

Modern-Day Shepherds

+ Billups writes, "There *are* modern-day shepherds in our midst. People who do the hard work, who are willing to take late-night shifts. I wonder if instead of herding sheep they herd people: men and women working late nights and probably not expecting anything spectacular to happen in their ordinary lives" (page 98). She specifically mentions Uber drivers. Who else might be considered current-day shepherds? Who are some people who do essential jobs—including jobs that are dangerous or unforgiving—but who don't get much glory or recognition?

+ When have you felt overlooked or as though your work was unappreciated?

+ Think about everything that is a part of your day-to-day life: food, transportation, a place to live or work, and so on. What people play a role in making these things possible? Consider people you've never seen or met.

+ What could you do to show appreciation to these current-day shepherds who are so important to your life? (*Note*: Showing appreciation isn't limited to giving gifts or recognizing people in a public setting. Appreciation could involve things such as learning someone's name, saying hello, saying thanks, finding little ways to make a person's job easier, and so on.) Which of these things could you do in the coming week?

+ Luke tells us that, after the shepherds saw Jesus, "they spread the word concerning what had been told them about this child" (page 101). The shepherds were the first people tasked with telling the Christmas story. What current-day shepherds have been responsible for telling you the story of Jesus?

+ The shepherds were unlikely recipients of God's call to visit the Christ child and spread the word of his birth. They also received this call at an unlikely time: at night while they were working. When have you encountered God or experienced God's presence in an unlikely time or place?
+ What can we do to prepare ourselves to encounter God anywhere and at any time?

When God Shows Up

+ Read Matthew 1:23. Matthew cites a verse from Isaiah and refers to Jesus as *Immanuel*, which means, "God with us." In Jesus, to quote Billups, God became "flesh and blood and moved into the neighborhood." For you, what is the significance of God living among humans in a fully human body?
+ Christians affirm that Jesus lived a fully human life on earth. We also affirm that Christ lives and is present with us all the time. In what ways do you experience God's presence during the Advent and Christmas seasons?
+ As followers of Christ, we tell our story using the seasons. Many of us feel especially close to God during our celebrations of Christmas and Easter, but don't always feel this same closeness at the other times of the year. Do you experience God differently at this time of year than you do during other times of the year? If so, how?
+ When do you struggle to feel God's presence?
+ Billups says of experiencing the presence of God, "It is not hocus-pocus, but you have to be focused" (page 105). In what ways do you focus on God's presence? What things keep you from focusing on God's presence?

+ Billups specifically names prayer and meditation as ways to focus. What is your experience with prayer? Is prayer something you do spontaneously when the need or urge arises? Is it part of a daily routine? Is it both?

+ What is your approach to prayer? Are there certain things you typically pray for? Do you do most of the talking? Do you strive to listen to the word that God has for you?

+ What challenges do you face when you pray? When is prayer difficult? When do you struggle to listen to or focus on God? What things in your life distract you from prayer and spending time alone with God?

+ What is your experience with meditation?

+ If you have experience with meditation, what effect did it have on your stress level and mental health? What effect did it have on your physical health? What effect did it have on your ability to focus?

+ Billups mentions lighting a candle on her desk to open herself to the movement of the Holy Spirit. In what other ways might you engage your senses to maintain your focus during prayer and meditation?

Unlikely Signs Through Unlikely People

Invite a volunteer to read aloud Luke 2:25-38.

+ The Christmas story is full of unlikely heroes. We've studied some of them so far: Elizabeth and Zechariah, the magi, and the shepherds. Billups also mentions Anna and Simeon. Who were Anna and Simeon? Why might they be considered unlikely witnesses of Jesus's birth?

+ Who are some other characters from the Gospels whom we might consider unlikely servants of God and followers

of Christ? (Examples might include: Zacchaeus the tax
collector, Luke 19:1-10; Nicodemus the Pharisee,
John 3:1-21; and the unnamed Canaanite woman,
Matthew 15:21-28.)

Anyone but Dorcas

Ask a volunteer to read aloud Acts 9:36-43.

+ This theme of God working through unlikely people
  continues throughout the Gospels and into the Acts of
  the Apostles, which serves as a sequel to Luke's Gospel.
  Who is the unlikely hero from this story in Acts?
+ What do these verses tell us about Tabitha, also known as
  Dorcas? What do they say about her role in the community?
+ Billups describes Dorcas as an "amazing servant." Who
  are some of the amazing servants in our congregation and
  community? What can we learn from their example?

Your Unlikely Story

+ When and how has God shown up in what the author refers
  to as your "dark nights and ordinary days" (page 110)? When
  have you experienced God amid stress or exhaustion or
  when you weren't in the mood?
+ Earlier in this session, we discussed the things that keep
  us from focusing on God. This can be especially true
  in the weeks leading up to Christmas. Many of us get
  busy and neglect the little things that keep us focused
  on our relationships with God and God's people. What
  is something small you can do when things get busy and
  stressful so that you don't neglect your spiritual practices
  or lose sight of how the Spirit is working in your life? (For
  example, this could be something as simple as saying a short

phrase or verse or making time for a ten-minute break. It might also involve writing a note to ourselves or posting a small reminder that the Holy Spirit is with us amid the chaos.)

Ask a volunteer to read aloud Isaiah 9:6.

+ Christians have long considered this verse a description of Jesus, the long-awaited Messiah. What does it mean for Christ to be a "Wonderful Counselor"? What does a counselor do and how does Jesus fill that role in our lives?
+ What does it mean for Christ to be the "Prince of Peace"? How does Christ bring peace both to our individual lives and to our world?
+ What things can we do this week, and during the remainder of the Christmas season, to "open our eyes and our schedules to God's presence" (page 111) as Billups writes?

Closing

Discuss:

+ What is one thing you learned during our time together that you didn't know before?
+ What is one thing that you will do in the coming week as a result of what we learned or discussed?

Closing Prayer

God, thank you for bringing us together for this time of study and discussion. Thank you for the witness of the shepherds. As we navigate the busyness of the season, give us the peace of mind to be aware of the Holy Spirit's constant presence in our lives. In Christ's name we pray. Amen.

Watch videos
based on
*An Unlikely Advent:
Extraordinary People
of the Christmas Story*
with Rachel Billups
through Amplify Media.

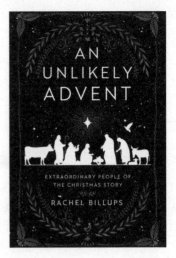

Amplify Media is a multimedia platform that delivers high quality, searchable content with an emphasis on Wesleyan perspectives for churchwide, group, or individual use on any device at any time. In a world of sometimes overwhelming choices, Amplify gives church leaders and congregants media capabilities that are contemporary, relevant, effective and, most importantly, affordable and sustainable.

With *Amplify Media* church leaders can:

- Provide a reliable source of Christian content through a Wesleyan lens for teaching, training, and inspiration in a customizable library
- Deliver their own preaching and worship content in a way the congregation knows and appreciates
- Build the church's capacity to innovate with engaging content and accessible technology
- Equip the congregation to better understand the Bible and its application
- Deepen discipleship beyond the church walls

**Ask your group leader or pastor about Amplify Media
and sign up today at www.AmplifyMedia.com.**